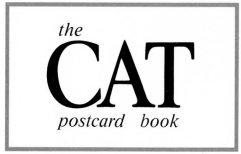

the
CAT
postcard book

RUNNING PRESS

PHILADELPHIA • PENNSYLVANIA

Postcard Book is a trademark of Running Press Book Publishers.

Canadian representatives: General Publishing Co., Ltd.,
30 Lesmill Road, Don Mills, Ontario M3B 2T6.
International representatives: Worldwide Media Services, Inc.,
115 East Twenty-third Street, New York, New York 10010.

9   8   7   6   5

The digit on the right indicates the number of this printing.

ISBN: 0-89471-519-4 (Paper)
Cover design by Toby Schmidt
Cover illustration: *Cat and Kittens,* c. 1872–1883; American;
National Gallery of Art, Washington/Gift of Edgar William and
Bernice Chrysler Garbisch.
Spine illustration: Detail of *Cat and Kittens.*
Back cover illustration: *Woman with a Cat,* c. 1875, by Pierre
Auguste Renoir; National Gallery of Art, Washington/Gift of
Mr. and Mrs. Benjamin E. Levy.

Special assistance: S. McDonough, V.M.D.

Typography by Comp-Art, Philadelphia, Pennsylvania
Printed and bound in the United States of America by Innovation Printing
This book can be ordered by mail from the publisher. Please add $2.50
postage and handling for each copy.
But try your bookstore first!

Running Press
Book Publishers
125 South Twenty-second Street
Philadelphia, Pennsylvania 19103

Cats—what is it about them that appeals to the artist?

Perhaps it's their eyes: now dagger-sharp and penetrating, now new-moons of contentment.

Maybe it's their range of attitudes: the hunter-cat, the regal cat, the cat asleep on the windowsill.

Or is it the fluid way these shape-shifting creatures carry themselves as they slink and pounce and curl themselves into drowsy bundles?

The subtlety of their temperament and their magnificence of form have earned cats a place in our hearts and at our hearths. We admire their independence, ponder their secrets (for surely they keep secrets from us), and indulge their idiosyncrasies.

The images in this book, created by artists from divergent cultures and different centuries, attest to the enduring appeal of the creature whose enigmatic personality stirs our curiosity. Here is a living creature that captivates and astonishes us like some mythological beast: here is the Cat.

Cats by Theophile-
Alexandre Steinlen (French,
b. Switzerland, 1859–1923).
Hand-colored lithograph.
Courtesy of the Museum
of Fine Arts, Boston/
Bequest of W. Russell
Allen.

The Arena by Harold
Weston (American, 1894–
1972). Oil on canvas. The
Phillips Collection,
Washington.

Cat, Rock, and Peonies,
18th century (Chinese).
Painting on silk. Courtesy
of the Freer Gallery of Art,
Smithsonian Institution,
Washington, D.C.,
Acc. No. 09.245r.

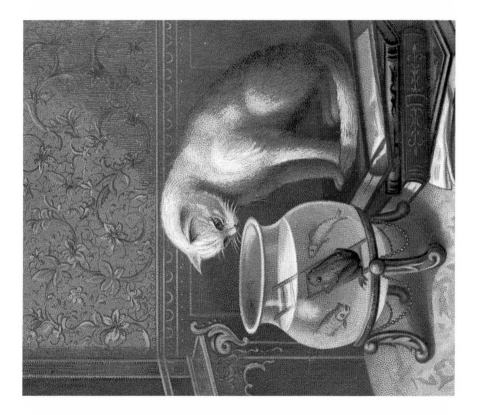

The Fisher, c. 1885, by
Raphael Tuck and Sons
(British), Chromo-
lithograph. Hallmark
Historical Collection,
Hallmark Cards, Inc.

Cat and Butterfly, Edo period, Ukiyo-e school, by Hokusai (Japanese, 1760–1849). Painting on paper. Courtesy of the Freer Gallery of Art, Smithsonian Institution, Washington, D.C., Acc. No. 02.42.

Minnie from the Outskirts of the Village, 1876, by R. P. Thrall (American). Oil on canvas. Courtesy of the Shelburne Museum, Shelburne, Vermont.

***Little White Kitties into
Mischief***, 1871, by Currier
& Ives (American). Hand-
colored lithograph.
Museum of the City of
New York/Harry T. Peters
Collection.

Rattown Tigers, 1894,
Louis Prang and Co., after
a painting by L.A.
DeRibas.
Chromolithograph.
Courtesy of the Boston
Public Library, Print
Department.

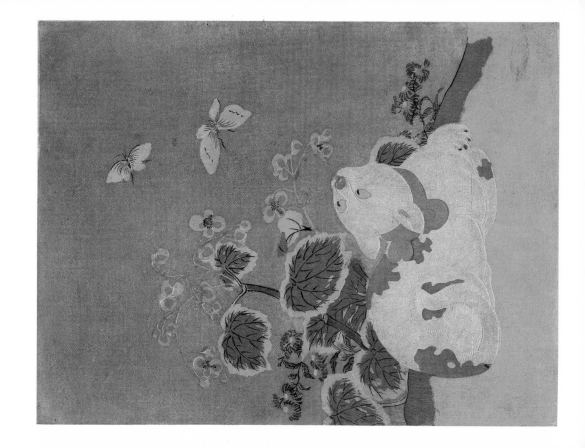

Cat, Butterfly, and Begonia
by Harunobu (Japanese,
1725?–1770). Woodblock
print. Museum of Art,
Rhode Island School of
Design/Gift of Mrs. John
D. Rockefeller, Jr.

Mischievous Kitty, 19th
century (American).
Advertising trade card for
E. G. Southwick & Co.
Northampton Historical
Society, Northampton,
Massachusetts.

Cat on the Floor, 1902, by Theophile-Alexandre Steinlen (French, b. Switzerland; 1859–1923). Soft ground etching, aquatint and drypoint. The Fine Arts Museum of San Francisco/Achenbach Foundation for Graphic Arts Purchase.

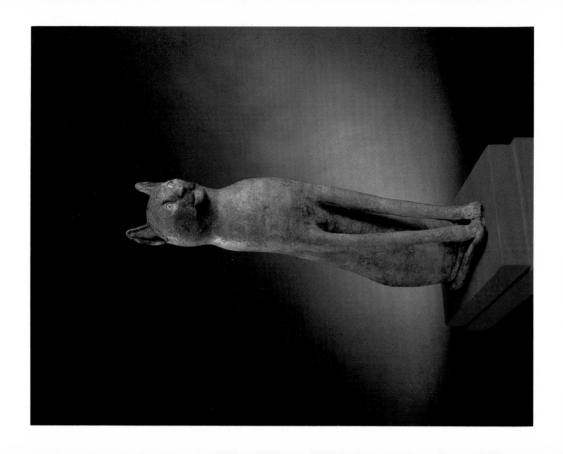

Cat, 22nd Dynasty, 945–715
B.C. (Egyptian). Bronze;
eyes inlaid with sheet gold.
The University Museum,
University of Pennsylvania.

Cat Bathing, Edo period,
Ukiyo-e School, by
Hiroshige (Japanese,
1797–1858). Painting on
paper. Courtesy of the
Freer Gallery of Art,
Smithsonian Institution,
Washington, D.C.,
Acc. No. 04.357.

E.B.W.

**Cats Looking Over a
Fence**, 1888, by Louis
Prang and Company
(American). Chromolitho-
graph. Hallmark Historical
Collection, Hallmark
Cards, Inc.

Cat and Kitten, 1986, by
Pamela Higgins Patrick
(American). Pastel on
paper.

Cat and Kittens,
c. 1872–1883 (American).
Oil on millboard. National
Gallery of Art, Washington/
Gift of Edgar William and
Bernice Chrysler Garbisch.

***View from a Window of
Visitors to Kinryuzan
Temple***, 1857, by Hiroshige
(Japanese, 1797–1858).
Woodblock print. Worcester
Art Museum, Worcester,
Massachusetts/John
Chandler Bancroft
Collection.

Winter: Cat on a Cushion,
1909, by Theophile-
Alexandre Steinlen (French,
b. Switzerland; 1859–1923).
Color lithograph. Jane
Voorhees Zimmerli Art
Museum, Rutgers, The
State University, New
Brunswick, New Jersey/
Class of 1958 Gift.

Playtime, c. 1885, by
Raphael Tuck and Sons
(British), Chromo-
lithograph. Hallmark
Historical Collection,
Hallmark Cards, Inc.

Tinkle, A Cat, April, 1883
(American). Oil on board;
reverse inscribed ''Tinkle
Born Febr. 1881!' Courtesy
of the Shelburne Museum,
Shelburne, Vermont.

Country Cat, 1986, by Reg Cartwright (British). Oil on masonite.

Naughty Puss!, 19th
century (American).
Advertising trade card for
Jayne's Tonic Vermifuge, a
cough remedy. Northamp-
ton Historical Society,
Northampton,
Massachusetts.

Sita and Sarita by Cecelia
Beaux (American, 1863–
1942). Oil on canvas. In the
collection of the Corcoran
Gallery of Art, Museum
Purchase, William A. Clark
Fund, 1923.

Girl with Cat, 1856, by
William Morris Hunt
(American, 1824–1879). Oil
on canvas. Courtesy of the
Museum of Fine Arts,
Boston/Bequest of
Edmund Dwight.

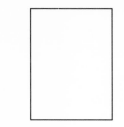

The Cat, c. 1840
(American). Oil on canvas.
National Gallery of Art,
Washington/Gift of Edgar
William and Bernice
Chrysler Garbisch.

**Summer: Cat on a
Balustrade**, 1909, by
Theophile-Alexandre
Steinlen (French, b.
Switzerland; 1859–1923).
Color lithograph. Jane
Voorhees Zimmerli Art
Museum, Rutgers, The
State University, New
Brunswick, New Jersey/
Class of 1958 15th
Anniversary Gift.

Woman with a Cat,
c. 1875, by Pierre Auguste
Renoir (French, 1841–1919).
Oil on canvas. National
Gallery of Art, Washington/
Gift of Mr. and Mrs.
Benjamin E. Levy.

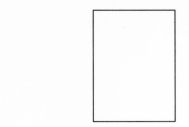

Still Life with Cat and Fish
by Jean Baptiste Siméon
Chardin (French, 1699–
1779). Oil on canvas. The
Nelson-Atkins Museum of
Art, Kansas City, Missouri/
Acquired through the
Anonymous Fund.

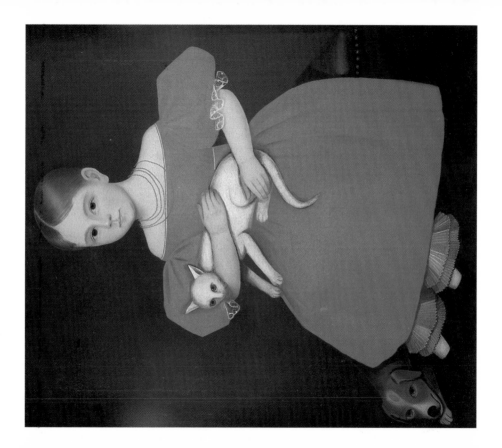

***Girl in Red with Her Cat
and Dog***, 1834–1836, by
Ammi Phillips (American,
1787 or 1788–1865). Oil on
canvas. From the perma-
nent collection of the
Museum of American Folk
Art.

Black Cat on a Chair by
Andrew L. von Wittkamp
(American, 19th century).
Oil on canvas. Courtesy of
the Museum of Fine Arts,
Boston/Bequest of Martha
C. Karolik for the Karolik
Collection of American
Paintings, 1815–1865.